YOUR KNOWLEDGE HAS VALUE

- We will publish your bachelor's and master's thesis, essays and papers

- Your own eBook and book -
  sold worldwide in all relevant shops

- Earn money with each sale

Upload your text at www.GRIN.com
and publish for free

Bibliographic information published by the German National Library:

The German National Library lists this publication in the National Bibliography; detailed bibliographic data are available on the Internet at http://dnb.dnb.de .

Imprint:

Copyright © 2017 GRIN Verlag, Open Publishing GmbH
Print and binding: Books on Demand GmbH, Norderstedt Germany
ISBN: 9783668552166

This book at GRIN:

http://www.grin.com/en/e-book/377453/factors-influencing-customers-perception-towards-online-shopping

Kunal Gaurav, Jhansi V.

Factors Influencing Customers' Perception towards Online Shopping

GRIN Publishing

GRIN - Your knowledge has value

Since its foundation in 1998, GRIN has specialized in publishing academic texts by students, college teachers and other academics as e-book and printed book. The website www.grin.com is an ideal platform for presenting term papers, final papers, scientific essays, dissertations and specialist books.

Visit us on the internet:

http://www.grin.com/

http://www.facebook.com/grincom

http://www.twitter.com/grin_com

Factors Influencing Customers' Perception towards Online Shopping

Dr. Kunal Gaurav
Associate Dean (Strategic Research)
ICBM – School of Business Excellence, Hyderabad – 500048, India

Ms. Jhansi V.
Student of PGDM (Batch of 2018)
ICBM – School of Business Excellence, Hyderabad – 500048, India

ICBM – School of Business Excellence
Hyderabad – 500048, India

Table of Contents

Abstract

Online shopping is having very bright future. Perception towards online shopping is getting better in India. With the use of internet, consumers can shop anywhere, anything and anytime with easy and safe payment options. Consumers can do comparison shopping between products, as well as, online stores. In present scenario customers are busy that they don't have enough chance and time to go to shopping centers and purchase the things they need, everybody likes to do online shopping. In online, Product assortment is very huge to choose, and make immediate comparison in price, quality, variety, colour and also get product based information like customer feedback.

The main purpose of this paper is to determine the **"Factors Influencing Consumer Perception towards Online Shopping".** The objective for this research is to know the customer perception and identify the factors which influence the online customer's.

A quantitative research design which is descriptive and exploratory in nature was selected to gain insights about customer perception towards online shopping. The questionnaire prepared by using Likert's five-point scale ranging from (1-5) where 1 Means 'not at all important and 5 Means 'most important '.The research has taken use of closed ended questions. The data collection was done over a period of 8 weeks this was done by going directly to the respondents or through mails. A total number of respondents taken for this study are 154. The collected data is analyzed in statistical method of factor analysis in the IBM SPSS 20.0 software. The data collected on 30 variables was deducted into five factors in the software and analyzed accordingly.

The survey revealed that different customers have different perception towards online shopping; most of them having a very good attitude towards online shopping but there are certain customer who still find difficulties or we can say apart from several benefits has some disadvantage in mind of customer. Customer perception keeps on changing with time to time which is to be taken in the consideration.The most important factors that can be taken into account to understand the Internet shopping (Customer Service, Convenience, Experience, Value added service and Product related information).

3

List of Tables

List of Figures

CHAPTER-1
Introduction

1.1: Overview

1.2: Objectives of the study

1.3: Scope of study

1.1: Introduction

Online shopping is the system whereby buyers purchase products or service from a seller in the real-time, over the Internet. It is a type of electronic business. The origin and growth of Internet have been the biggest event of the century. E-commerce in India was started in 1999 to a period where one can sell and find all sorts of stuff from a high-end product to a meagre peanut online. Most corporations are using the Internet to represent their product range and services so that it is accessible to the global market and to reach out to a larger range of their audience. The Internet has completely changed the way one handles day-to-day transactions; online shopping is one of them. The Internet has brought about extensive changes in the purchasing habits of the people. In the comfort of one's home, office or cyber cafe or anywhere across the world, one can log on and buy just about anything from apparel, books, music and diamond jeweler to digital cameras, mobile phones, MP3 players, video games, movie tickets, rail and air tickets. Ease, simplicity, convenience and security are the key factors turning the users to buy online.

The process of making a decision is extremely similar whether the customer is offline or online. But some major differences are shopping environment and marketing communication. According to traditional consumer decision model, Consumer purchase decision typically starts with need awareness, then information search, alternative evaluations, deciding to purchase and finally, post-purchasing behavior.

As far as online, when customers see standard advertisements or online promotion, these advertisements may pull in customers' attention and stimulate their interest for specific items. Before they decide to buy, they will require extra information to help them out. On the offline shore they don't have enough chance to know the information; they will look through online channels, e.g., online lists, sites, or web indexes. Whenever customers have enough information, they should look at to compare those choices of products or services. In the search stage, they may search for the product reviews or customer comments. They will discover which brand or organization offers them the best fit to their desire. During this stage, the attractiveness of the web and the pleasing new collection or design is essential things to convince shoppers to be interested in buying product and service the most helpful characteristic of online is that it supports the pre-purchase stage, as it helps a customer to think about various alternatives. During the buying stage, product assortment, sale services and information quality appear to be the most vital point to help a customer to choose what item they should choose, or what seller they should purchase from. Post-purchase behavior will turn out to be more crucial after their online buying. Consumers sometimes have a problem or concern about the product, or they might want to change or return the product that they have bought. Thus, return and exchange services turn out to be essential at this stage.

RajanAnandan, VP & Managing Director of Google India (2013); said "With approximately 8 million Indians shopping online in 2012, online shopping industry in India is growing rapidly and will continue to see exponential growth. By looking at the trends in 2012, we expect 2013 to be a strong growth year for players who're focused on fast-growing categories like apparels & accessories and niche product categories like baby products, home furnishings & health-nutrition. We expect the growth to come from outside of top 8 metros as was evident in ourrecently concluded 'Great Online Shopping Festival' which saw over 51% of traffic from non-metros."[1]

According to Internet World Stats in March 2017, India has the second largest number of internet users in Asia after China having a 24.7 percent of users. Based on the Internet Live Stats, India's count of internet users has been increasing at a rate of 4963% from 2000 to 2017[2]. This large internet user base will have a direct effect on the Indian online shopping business. In fact, Google India mentions that around 55 million Indians purchases products online and this number is rising every year. The swift increase in the usage of the internet over the past two decades, as a place for buyer-seller dealings, is significant of the extent of recognition of online transactions. The growth of e-commerce industry has led to a sizeable increase in the online transactions. According to the Associated Chambers of Commerce and Industry of India (Assocham), the size of the e-commerce industry is likely to grow at an annual rate of 25% to Rs.2500crore by 2017[3]. The online industry has seen a jump in the number of transactions with the change in the consumer buying behavior from a physical store to an online store.

This extraordinary increase in the online transactions is due to advances in technology, changing behavior patterns of the consumers and sometimes situational influences. Shopping online is generally defined as the idea of buying and selling of products over the internet. The

[1]http://bestmediainfo.com/2013/01/online-shopping-set-for-exponential-growth-in-2013-google-india/(accessed on 1st July 2017)
[2]http://www.internetworldstats.com/stats.htm(accessed on 1st July 2017)
[3]http://www.assocham.org/newsdetail.php?id=5427(accessed on 1st July 2017)

sellers' viewpoint is to convince and catch the attention of the prospective consumers' to purchase products and make sure that he/she is satisfied. The buyers' outlook towards online shopping is the extent to which he/she can access, browse, purchase, transact and repeat the same behavior. In this digital age, consumers are driven by the technology. They are searching for the product on the internet and eventually buying it. Sometimes there are a lot of hesitations and doubts while shopping online. Some of the most prominent ones being risk involved in sharing financial and personal information, inability to touch and try the goods before purchasing and concerns related to not getting the right product.

Customer perception is a marketing concept that encompasses a customer's impression, awareness and consciousness about a company or its offerings. Perception is the process by which we select, organize, and interpret information inputs to create a meaningful picture of the world. A customer's perception is affected by advertising, reviews, public relation, social media, personal experience and other factors. In general, perception is gathering information through seeing, hearing, touching, tasting, smelling and sensing. Perception is the process by which these stimuli are selected, organized, and interpreted. Customer perception enables the marketing manager to understand how the customer views a product or service and then formulate the strategy accordingly.

At this backdrop, this study was decided to understand the customers' perception towards online shopping.

1.2: Objectives of the study

- To understand the consumers' perception towards online shopping.
- To identify the factors influencing the consumers' perception towards online shopping.

1.3 Scope of the Study

From this study, one can get knowledge about what factors influence customers' perceptions, their attitude towards a product and services.This study helps to know about the opinion of the customer about online shopping. It helps the online shops to carry out their business successfully by understanding customers' perception, taste and preference towards products and services offered at the online shops.

CHAPTER-2

Review of Literature

2. Review of Literature

E-Retail has changed and expanded in all lines of business, be it apparel, jewellery, footwear, Groceries, electronics etc. In today's competitive world, with increasing number of online retail stores, the retailers need to be more customer-oriented.Indian businesses need to understand the changing behaviour of customers towards shopping in organised wed sites. The focus of much of the research is on the 'disconfirmation of expectations' theory which explains that "the customer is satisfied when he or she feels that the product's performance is equal to more than what was expected (confirmation). But if the perceived performance falls short of his/her expectations (disconfirmation), then the customer is dissatisfied". And also website design, website reliability, customer service and privacy are the four key factors which influence consumers' perceptions of online shopping(Alamosa, 2011).

Sarigiannidis&Maditinos (2011) explains that around half the internet users have bought a product or service through the internet and according to (Li and Zhang, 2002); online shopping is the third most well-liked internet activity. Most of them have tried to identify factors that affect or contribute to online consumer behaviour. Researchers seem to adopt different points of view and focus on different factors in different ways.

A study done by Indian Institute of E-commerce, according to that by 2020 India is expected to produce $100 billion online retail revenue. Out of which nearly $35 billion will be through fashion e-commerce. Online apparel sales are set to grow four times in coming years. (Marie, 2005); discussed how consumers react and behave with respect to the e-commerce in India which is at the very nice in stages to as competitive western world, if you look at the e-commerce in India are we are a 16-billion-dollar market in India within 3504 million users growing at the rate of 34% in the last five years so it is becoming huge in India.In India where we can buy anything from a mobile phone, charger, Sim card, groceries, to personal care products (Fiore, Kim, & Lee,2007).

12

The rise of the Internet has moved trade into an electronic age, changing practically every part of the day to day lives, from how shoppers convey and find out about item offerings, to how they shop and purchase items and administrations. Obviously, publicising through the Internet is currently an essential wellspring of purchase data. The Internet is the quickest developing retail channel, with deals volumes about triple that of aggregate retail deals in 2004. Web retail deals are anticipated to reach over $331 billion by 2010. In spite of the current monetary hardship testing shoppers around the world, the expanding selection of the Internet among the overall public seems to extend a brighter future for retail Internet patronization by customers. Purchasers progressively are utilising the Internet to gather e-coupons and make their own particular virtual coupon books, who guarantee that buyers acquire online an assortment of coupons, from shopping for food to theatre exhibitions to lodgings (Kumar, Anand &Mutha,2016)

The continuous growth of electronic commerce constitutes a unique opportunity for companies to replace traditional "brick and mortar" stores with virtual ones and to reach customers more efficiently and in a larger geographical area. The modern train which recalls Wal-Mart in the western and we have big bazaar, food Bazaar, Spencer's in India which is still very small but growing in e-commerce or a market place is my nude as compared to these two but slowly gaining a lot of traction and it is kind of become an integrated retail outlet place for formulating their distribution strategy, however, the e-commerce place works very different understanding of consumers and how they make their online buying decision (Nalchigar& Weber,2012).

In India Mobile, access over 250 million in that 130 million are the active users from rural area and over 40 million of consumers are online and nearly 20 million people purchase from online. In the year 2013 (Google India and TNS Australia) undertook a study to get a deeper insight into the key drivers of online shopping and saw 128% growth in the internet users in the year 2012-13, which is only 40% in the year 2010-11. The study indicates validating the growth in trends, 9 out of 10 e-commerce buyers intend to spend more on online shopping (Hasan, &Mishra, 2014).

The greater contribution from non-metros a greater number of queries will originate from the mobile phone, now a day's which become an indispensable tool which has changed the lifestyle of people (Xu, 2005).

Now a day's customers are more attracted towards foreign brands, those global brands which may not be accessible to the bricks & mortar formats but are becoming more accessible to the e-commerce platforms this is also the consumer base which is a big Smartphone usage almost every second audience in this age group today owns a Smartphone which is becoming one of the major factors towards the promotion of e-commerce in this age group (Park, 2003).

Fiore, Niehm, & Lorenz (2009) has explained that in online, Product assortment is very huge to choose, and make immediate comparison in price, quality, variety, colour and the other two important factors which are affecting Indian market that nobody wants to pay for the shipping of the product but in India is typically a bigger issue, when a consumer sees that they are being made to pay for the shipping it takes to move out of the platform immediately. However, if they have a free shipping option they are basically more ready to take the risk because they're still in that initial stage of purchase decision where they are learning the platform. And try to assimilate the platform so free shipping becomes very critical and cash on delivery (Goswami, 2015).

In tire 2 and tire 3 towns who don't have access to debit cards, they cannot make transactions online and cash on delivery, therefore, become a critical challenge for them. No of housewives, students, who want to follow new trends and experiment with global brands are upset because they may not have the credit cards, but they still want to see the products and for them cash on delivery becomes a very good option, also we are very risk averse kind of consumers who like to see a product, touch the product, feel the product, before they really pay for it. Still, many internet customers avoid purchasing online due to privacy and security concern they still hesitation to send personal information through the internet. So, even if they have access to the credit card having online transaction facility, they still hesitant to pay for something which they don't have in hands. So the cash on delivery and free shipping options become one of the major factors to influence the customer online buying decision (Jusoh&Ling 2012).

Darley, Blankson, &Luethge (2010) conclude that there is a huge gap of research on the impact of online environments on decision making. According to a 2008 report on "Online Shopping" from Pew Internet and American Life Project (a leading non-profit authority on Internet usage trends), almost 80% of customers say that the Internet is the best place to buy items that are hard to find. But at the same time, almost 60% of customer also says that they get irritated, confused, or overwhelmed while searching for the complete product information.

Ha &Stoel (2009) has explained factors influencing customer acceptance of online shopping. The outcome of the study suggests that online quality consists of four dimensions: (1) website design, (2) customer service, (3) privacy/security, and (4) atmospheric/experiential. that explained variance of the first factor, website design (51.51 percent), is greater than the other three factors, accounting for the greatest proportion of variation in overall perceptions of e-shopping quality positive perceptions of e-shopping quality predict consumers' beliefs about ease of use, shopping enjoyment, and trust. The study also reveals technology acceptance behaviour for users within the context of online shopping. The finding that trust and enjoyment perceptions play considerable roles in consumers' adoption of e-shopping supports previous research. In comparing path coefficients of antecedents of attitudetoward shopping, usefulness emerges as the most powerful predictor of attitude toward e-shopping relative to the other belief factors.

Zhou, Dai & Zhang (2007) has conducted a general survey of extant related studies and synthesised their findings into a reference model called OSAM (Online Shopping Acceptance Model) to explain consumer acceptance of online shopping. This study reveals that a countless of factors have been examined in the area of online shopping and mixed results on those factors have been reported. The research also identified highlights a few managerial issues that should be appealing to online retailers. The projected model helps to resolve conflicting findings, discover recent trends in this line of research, and show the new directions to the future research.

The ascent of the Internet has moved trade into an electronic age, changing practically every part of day to day lives, from how shoppers convey and find out about item offerings, to how they shop and purchase items and administrations. Obviously, publicising through the Internet is currently an essential wellspring of purchase data. The Internet is the quickest developing retail channel, with deals volumes about triple that of aggregate retail deals in 2004. Web retail deals are anticipated to reach over $331 billion by 2010. In spite of the current monetary hardship testing shoppers around the world, the expanding selection of the Internet among the overall public seems to extend a brighter future for retail Internet patronization by customers. Purchasers progressively are utilising the Internet to gather e-coupons and make their own particular virtual coupon books, who guarantee that buyers acquire online an assortment of coupons, from shopping for food to theatre exhibitions to lodgings (Swarnakar & Kumar 2016).

Taking fashion to the online market is a dramatic move in this social experience. The absence of helpful staff and lack of touch feel can also challenge this experience particularly that fashion products are heterogeneous in nature. the importance of modern technologies in advancing the online shopping environment for fashion sites and creates them in the more attractive way. Hence, the social dimension of fashion shopping might be met through modern technology. He explained that with regards to fashion shopping, image interactivity, image zooming and 360-degree rotation increase shopping enjoyment and trim down perceived risk toward the online retailer (Nalchigar, & Weber, 2012).

Kim and Lennon (2010) investigated the influence of further product presentation features such as the use of a model (as opposed to flat display) and colour swapping on clothing in addition to image zooming. Because of the inability to try the apparel products before purchase, online product presentation will play an important in the context of online apparel stores". Fashion behaviour is deeply rooted in emotional and psychological motivations new features implemented on different websites include links to share outfits on social media sites as well as facebook groups and pages where customers have the ability to chat and share thoughts on the particular brand or piece of clothes of interest. Also, some websites started to implement chat with advisor facility which offers the opportunity to speak to an advisor as in offline stores. That can enhance the effectiveness of a Web-based sales channel. That is, having the choice to chat with an advisor may result in a more successful apparel website. Shopper attitude is influenced by visual and verbal information about the product of interest. However, verbal information seems to have the main influence of shopper intention.

Burke, R.R. (2002), Trust is a key component that decides the accomplishment of Business to Consumer (B2C) online business exchanges. Past specialists have distinguished a few basic considerations that impact believes the setting of online shopping. This exploration concentrates on accessible safety efforts which guarantee online customers security and incredible deals advancements and online arrangements which invigorate clients to shop on the web.

The absence of trust in online exchanges has been referred to as the primary explanation behind the severe dislike of web-based shopping. We have tried the intervening part of trust in online exchanges to give observational proof that trust in the online store speaks to the band instrument through which the central free factors of web architecture can emphatically impact buy aim and diminish the apparent hazard. We have additionally shown the directing impact of the person's way of life in online business and in this way offered experiences into the relative significance of web composition variables adding to trust for clients of various social esteems, (Ganguly, 2010).

Marios&Sosa, (2004)revealed that absence of trust in online companies is a major reason why a lot of customers don't prefer online shopping. This study proposes a model that explains how new customers of an online company build up initial trust in the company after their first online visit. The model is empirically tested using a questionnaire-based field study. The results show that previous company reputation and readiness to modify products and services can significantly affect initial trust. Perceived website usefulness, ease of use, and security control are also a significant experience of initial trust. Finally, they found no support for the hypothesised result of individual customer trust propensity on initial trust.

Trust has been exactly settled as one of the keys ascribes in business to client (B2C) web based business. The impact of measures to manufacture and keep up confides in B2C Online Shopping is liable to client drove conduct variables, which can be controlled by the business firm. The present investigation directed in the Indian setting investigates the part of shopper .self-viability and site social nearness in client & selection of B2C web based shopping intervened by confiding in saw value, and saw hazard. The most critical result of the investigation is that the shopper self-adequacy and site social-nearness influence put stock in, saw helpfulness and saw hazard in the online clients, and thusly emphatically impact the client's goal to buy items on the web(Dash,&Saji, 2007).

Throughout the years the advancement of the Internet as a showcasing medium has turned into a worldwide marvel. The ascent in the quantity of family units having a computer and the simplicity of Internet get to have prompted this far-reaching acknowledgement of web based business. The absence of trust in online exchanges has been referred to, by past researchers, as the primary explanation behind the extreme a version of Internet shopping. In this paper, we proposed a model and gave observational confirmation on the effect of the site attributes on to confide in online exchanges in the Indian setting. In the main stage, we recognised and experimentally confirmed the relative significance of the site figures that create online trust in India. In the following stage, we have tried the arbiter impact of trust in the connection between the site variables and buy the goal (and saw chance). The present examination interestingly gave exact proof on the intervening part of trust in web-based shopping among Indian clients (Ganguly, 2010).

Abel Stephen (2003) in his paper speaks to the discoveries of research considers that address internet business outline and related customer conduct. The development of internet business has influenced not just the commercial centre through the help of the trading of products and enterprises, additionally human conduct in light of the instruments of online administrations. Specialists have distinguished and guessed on applicable topics going from Web ease of use, promoting stations and different elements affecting web based purchasing conduct. In spite of the fact that scientists have concentrated on what seem diverse parts of internet purchasing conduct, their examinations might be appeared to be interrelated and associated, even to the degree of uncovering develops whereupon web based business, as far as future outline and research, could be constructed.

Subramanian, & Konan (2003), explained some conventional administration quality measurements that decide consumer loyalty, for example, the physical appearance of offices, workers, and hardware, and representative's responsiveness and sympathy are inconspicuous. Interestingly, a trust may assume a focal part here in upgrading consumer loyalty. Show trust as an endogenously shaped element that at last effects consumer loyalty, and we clarify the linkages amongst trust and different elements identified with the execution of the online specialist organisation and to the administration condition.

Customer contributions in internet purchase have turned into a very important pattern. Thusly, it is essential to recognise the customer online purchase intention. The aim of the study is to measure the effects of shopping orientation, online trust and earlier online shopping experience and understand the customer online purchase intention. a study of 242 undergraduate students from a private college in Malaysia taken for this research The study revealed that impulse purchase intention, quality orientation, brand orientation, online trust and prior online purchase experience were completely related to the customer online purchase intention (Chai, Ling, &Piew,2010)

Kamineni, (2004) in his examination finds that World Wide Web can change human conduct and human connections to an expensive degree. Online shopping conduct is one noteworthy case to bring up the patterns toward this path. This examination is of an exceptionally exploratory nature and it expects to build up the contrasts between a few online customers from various parts of the world. A few basic components related to web based shopping conduct have been investigated. A multifaceted informational index has been gathered and an illustrative portrayal of the customers has been given. As the last stride, the culturally diverse contrasts between a few customers investigated.

Shrivastava, &Lanjewar, (2011) in web-based purchasing, the rate of dissemination and selection of the web based purchasing among shoppers is still moderately low in India. In perspective of above issue, an experimental investigation of web based purchasing conduct was attempted. In light of writing survey, four prevalent psychographic parameters to be specific state of mind, inspiration, identity, and trust were contemplated as for web based purchasing. The internet purchasing choice process models in view of all the four parameters were composed after the factual investigation. These models were incorporated with business insight, learning administration and information mining to plan Behavioral Business

19

Intelligence structure with a firm perspective of online purchase conduct. For better understanding the components of web and buyer shopping practices towards web shopping, this section would give scholastic research surveys and relative thoughts communicated in the writing that related to this subject. Besides, various speculations will be tried to answer the exploration addresses that said as of now in the presentation. Because of the current research demonstrates that web shopping turns into a full and powerful plan of action in this way there are a few examinations that as of now explored pretty much related to web shopping and buyer conduct. In the accompanying section, some perspective will be taken from written works and needs cautious audit to accomplish them as the premise of the consequent research examination(Dasgupta, & Smith, 2005).

Punj(2012) explains that purchase can possibly only when to improve quality products are available in the online. But whether such potential is being acknowledged by most customers is an uncertain matter. Subsequently, the motivation behind this exploration is to see how (1) certain elements of electronic situations favourably affect the abilities of consumers to settle on better choices, and (2) identify information-processing strategies that would empower the customer to settle on better quality choices while shopping on the web. A cross-disciplinary theoretical analysis based on constructs drawn from financial aspects (e.g., time costs), processing (e.g., suggestion specialists), and brain science (e.g., choice systems) are directed to distinguish elements that possibly impact choice quality in an electronic environment. The research is important from a theoretical point of view because it examines an important aspect of online consumer decision making, namely, the impact of the electronic environment on the abilities of customers. The research is important from a hypothetical point of view since it looks at an essential part of online purchase decision making, in particular, the effect of the electronic environment on the abilities of customers. It is essential from both a managerial and public policy point of view on the grounds that the capacity of customers to settle on the better-quality decision while shopping online is directly related to improving market efficiency and improving customer welfare in electronic markets.

CHAPTER-3

Research Methodology

3.1 Type of research

3.2 Sampling Unit

3.3 Sampling Technique

3.4 Questionnaire Design

3.5 Data Collection Sources

3.6 Plan for Data analysis

3.1 Type of research

A quantitative research design which is descriptive and exploratory in nature was selected to gain insights about customers' perception towards online shopping.

3.2 Sampling Unit

The sampling unit for the study is individuals who prefer online shopping. The survey is made, keeping in mind different economic groups like people of low class, middle class and high class. The survey is also made, keeping in mind all classes of people such as business persons, house wives, students, government employees& private employees. The size of the sample extends to 154 respondents (Refer Appendix II for Sample Profile).

3.3 Sampling Technique

Convenience sampling method is adopted because data collection is done from the population members who are conveniently available to participate in the survey.

3.4 Questionnaire Design

Questionnaire development is the critical part of primary data collection method. The questions were framed in a sample manner, capable of being answered easily and quickly by the respondents. The questionnaire was designed using various scaling techniques. The questionnaire was used mainly to understand consumer perception towards online shopping. this questionnaire prepared by usingLikert's five-point scale ranging from (1-5) where 1 Means 'not at all important,2 Means 'unimportant', 3 Means 'neither important nor unimportant', 4 Means ' important', And 5 Means 'most important'.

3.5 Data Collection Sources

As a part of data analysis both primary and secondary data has been collected.

Primary data: Here the data is collected to obtain desired information through structured questionnaire.

Secondary data: Secondary data for this project is collected from the company's website and online research papers published in journals.

3.6 Data Collection

The research has taken use of closed ended questions.The data collection was done over a period of 8 weeks; this was done by going directly to the respondents or through mails.

3.7 Plan for Data analysis

The collected data is analyzed with the help of factor analysis by IBM SPSS 20.0 software. The data collected on 30 variables was deducted into five factors in the software and analyzed accordingly. The technique of Varimax rotation was used to maximize the sum of the variances of the squared loadings.

CHAPTER-4

Data Analysis and Interpretation

4.1 Factor Analysis
4.2 Net Promoter Score
4.3 Frequency Analysis

4.1 Factor Analysis

Factor analysis is a multivariate statistical method of data reduction, which is usually used in psychology, education, and more recently in the health-related professions.
It has many uses, three of which will be briefly noted here.

1. Factor analysis reduces a large number of variables into a smaller set of variables.
2. It establishes fundamental dimensions between calculated variables and dormant constructs, thereby allowing the formation and refinement of theory.
3. It provides construct validity evidence of self-reporting scales.

Factor analysis is used to distinguish latent elements or factors. It is normally used to decrease variables into a smaller set to save time and encourage less demanding understandings. There are many extraction techniques for example, Principal Axis Factor and Maximum Likelihood. Factor analysis isnumerically intricate and the criteria used to decide the number and essentialness of variables are vast. There are two sorts of rotation techniques – orthogonal rotation and oblique rotation. Orthogonal rotation (e.g., Varimax and Quartimax) includes uncorrelated factors through oblique rotation (e.g., Direct Oblimin and Promax) includes correlated factors. The interpretation of factor analysis is based on rotated factor loadings, rotated eigenvalues, and scree test. In reality, researchers often use more than one extraction and rotation technique based on practicalanalysis rather than hypotheticalanalysis.

Factor Analysis model

If the variables are standardized, the factor model can be represented as:

$X_i = A_{i1}F_1 + A_{i2}F_2 + A_{i3}F_3 + \ldots\ldots\ldots + A_{im}F_m + V_iU_i$

Where,

$X_i = i_{th}$ standardized vriable

A_{ij} = standardized multiple regression coefficient of variable i on common factor j

F = common factor

V_i = standardized regression coefficient of variable I on unique factor i

U_i = the unique factor for variable i

m = number of common factors

The unique factors are uncorrelated with each other and with the common factors. The commonfactors themselves can be expressed as linear combinations of the observed variables

$F_i = W_{i1}X_1 + W_{i2}X_2 + W_{i3}X_3 + \ldots\ldots\ldots + W_{ik}X_k$

Where,

F_i = estimate of i_{th} factor

W_i = weight or factor score coefficient

k = number of variables.

4.1.1 KMO and Bartlett's Test

Kaiser-Meyer-Olkin Measure of Sampling Adequacy.		.851
Bartlett's Test of Sphericity	Approx. Chi-Square	1900.043
	Df	435
	Sig.	.000

Kaiser-Meyer-Olkin(KMO) Measure of Sampling Adequacy examines the suitability of factor analysis. This measure fluctuates between 0 and 1, and values between 0.5 and 1 indicate that factor analysis is appropriate. KMO acquired for this analysis is .851(>0.5). Thus, factor analysis can be considered. we can see that the Bartlett's Test of Sphericity is significant (0.000). That is, significance is less than 0.05. This means that correlation matrix is an identity matrix.

4.1.2 Communalities

The output is a table of communalities which shows how much of the variance (i.e. the communality value which should be more than 0.3 to be considered for further analysis. Else these variables are to be removed from further steps factor analysis) in the variables has been accounted for by the extracted factors.

	Initial	Extraction
10.Convenience of buying anytime anywhere	1.000	.493
11.Range of products	1.000	.642
12.Price dynamism	1.000	.630
13.Ability to compare products	1.000	.401
14.Availability of Value for money products	1.000	.497
15.Products matching online description	1.000	.502
16.On time delivery of the products	1.000	.554
17.Availability of International brands	1.000	.454
18.Detailed view or image zooming	1.000	.530
19.Size guides(picture, table & test)	1.000	.629
20.Filter according to your preference	1.000	.540
21.Availability of trendy products	1.000	.384
22.Guarantee & Warranty associated with the offerings	1.000	.577
23.Information and review	1.000	.551
24.The overall website experience	1.000	.572
25.The attractiveness of the shopping portal	1.000	.356
26.The website is easy to navigate	1.000	.527

27.Discount & Coupon	1.000	.780
28.Gift wrapping facility	1.000	.550
29.images/videos of the product give a good sense of the actual product.	1.000	.416
30.Cash on delivery	1.000	.605
31.Easy to contact the customer service staff via email or chat	1.000	.458
32.Free shipping	1.000	.555
33.The online support staff is responsive to your needs	1.000	.434
34.Easy to replacement & return	1.000	.620
35.Product tracking facility	1.000	.566
36.Security of payment credentials	1.000	.625
37.EMI facility	1.000	.493
38.In time refund	1.000	.697
39.Standard delivery option	1.000	.561

Extraction Method: Principal Component Analysis.

4.1.3Total Variance Explained

The next item shows all the factors extractable from the analysis along with their eigenvalues.Eigenvalue actually reflects the number of extracted factors whose sum should be equal to number of items which are subjected to factor analysis. From the below table information, it is evident that out of the total extraction value of 53.994, thesignificant variability is found in the factors customer service and convenience. The value of rotated variance for Instant customer service is19.269 and the rotated variance forconvenience is 10.272.

Rotation Sums of Squared Loadings			
Component	Total	% of Variance	Cumulative %
1	5.781	19.269	19.269
2	3.082	10.272	29.541
3	2.849	9.497	39.039
4	2.490	8.299	47.338
5	1.997	6.656	53.994

Extraction Method: Principal Component Analysis.

Extraction Method: Principal Component Analysis.

4.1.4 Scree Plot

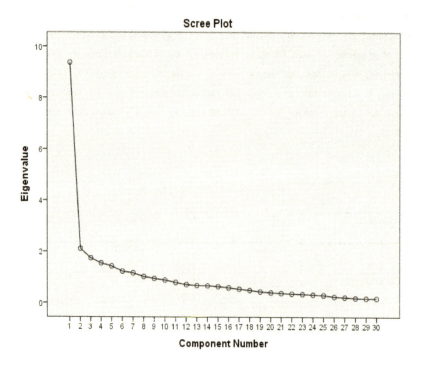

Scree Plot

The scree plot is a graphical representation of the eigenvalues against all the factors. The graph is helpful for determining how many factors to keep. The point of interest is that where the curve begins to flatten. It can be seen that the curve begins to flatten between factors 6 and 7. Note also that factor 6 onwards have an eigenvalue of less than 1, so only 5 factors have been retained.

4.1.5 Rotated Component Matrix

The table representing the loading of 30 variables into these five factors that helps in understanding the customers' perception towards online shopping is given below. The idea of rotation is to decrease the number factors on which the variables under investigation have high loadings. Rotation does not actually change anything but makes the interpretation of the analysis easier. Looking at the table below, largest factor loadings were considered for each of the items. All other variables are loaded on only one factor out of five factors.

	Component				
	Customer service	Convenience	Experience	Value added service	Product related information
On time delivery of the products	.475				
Guarantee & Warranty associated with the offerings	.721				
Information and review	.564				
The website is easy to navigate	.254				
images/videos of the product give a good sense of the actual product.	.511				
Easy to contact the customer service staff via email or chat	.601				
The online support staff is responsive to your needs	.605				
Easy to replacement & return	.642				
Product tracking facility	.521				
Security of payment credentials	.705				
EMI facility	.502				
In time refund	.818				
Standard delivery option	.675				

Convenience of buying anytime anywhere		.641		
Range of products		.774		
Price dynamism		.691		
Ability to compare products		.419		
Availability of Value for money products		.443		
Availability of International brands			.660	
Filter according to your preference			.446	
Availability of trendy products			.385	
The overall website experience			.601	
The attractiveness of the shopping portal			.524	
Discount & Coupon				.822
Gift wrapping facility				.643
Cash on delivery				.638
Free shipping				.503
Products matching online description					.491
Detailed view or image zooming					.575
Size guides(picture, table & test)					.466

Extraction Method: Principal Component Analysis.

Rotation Method: Varimax with Kaiser Normalization.

Factor Labelling and Interpretation

The factors (components) as obtained from the analysis were labelled under the following headings:

1. Customer Service
2. Convenience
3. Experience
4. Value added service
5. Product related information

Factor 1: Customer Service

From the above 30 variables, 13 variables are loaded in this factor. The percent of variance attributable to this factor after rotation is 19.269and the reliability of this factor, as measured by its Cronbach Alpha is 0.779(>.5) which indicates that the factor is reliable in explaining the variance in the factor. In the above all variable highest loaded value is "in time refund", that means online customers are more sensitive in money refund. All the variables loaded in this factor represents that the customer is more concern about the service while shopping in online portal.

4.1.6 Reliability Statistics

Cronbach's Alpha	N of Items
.779	13

Factor 2: Convenience

From the above 30 variables, 5 variables are loaded in this factor. The percent of variance attributable to this factor after rotation is 10.272 and the reliability of this factor, as measured by its Cronbach Alpha is 0.696(>.5) which indicates that the factor is reliable in explaining the variance in the factor. Convenient of the internet is one of the impacts on consumers' willingness to buy online. Online shopping is available for customers around the clock comparing to traditional store as it is open 24 hours a day, 7 days a week .Consumers not only look for products, but also for online services.

4.1.7 Reliability Statistics

Cronbach's Alpha	N of Items
.696	5

Factor 3: Experience

From the above 30 variables, 5 variables are loaded in this factor. The percent of variance attributable to this factor after rotation is 9.497 and the reliability of this factor, as measured by its Cronbach Alpha is 0.674(>.5) which indicates that the factor is reliable in explaining the variance in the factor. In the above all factors highest loaded factor is "Availability of International brands" it helps the customer to buy products from any corner of earth. Consumers not only look for products, but also for online services and experience.

4.1.8 Reliability Statistics

Cronbach's Alpha	N of Items
.674	5

Factor 4:Value added service

The variables loaded to this factor are "Discount & Coupon"," Gift wrapping facility"," Cash on delivery" & "Free shipping". The percent of variance attributable to this factor after rotation is 8.299 and the reliability of this factor, as measured by its Cronbach Alpha is 0.742(>.5) which indicates that the factor is reliable in explaining the variance in the factor. Variables loaded in this factor are motivating the customer to prefer online store rather than the traditional store.

4.1.9 Reliability Statistics

Cronbach's Alpha	N of Items
.742	4

Factor 5: Product related information

The variables loaded to this factor are "Products matching online description"," Detailed view or image zooming"& "Size guides(picture, table & test). The percent of variance attributable to this factor after rotation is 6.656 and the reliability of this factor, as measured by its Cronbach Alpha is 0.651(>.5) which indicates that the factor is reliable in explaining the variance in the factor. All these variables represent that, with the help of these feature customer can see the product more clearly, increase shopping enjoyment and trim down perceived risk toward the online retailer.

4.1.10 Reliability Statistics

Cronbach's Alpha	N of Items
.651	3

4.3 Net Promoter Score

Definition

The Net Promoter Score is ancatalog ranging from 0 to 10 that measures the readiness of customers to suggest a company's products or services to others. It is used as aalternative for gauging the customer's overall satisfaction with a company's product or service and the customer's loyalty to the brand.

In this method Customers are surveyed on one single question. They are asked to rate on an 11-point scale the likelihood of recommending the company or brand to a friend or family.

"On a scale of 0 to 10, how likely are you to recommend this company's product or service to a friend or a colleague?"

Based on the above parameters customers are classified in 3 categories: detractors, passives and promoters.

DETRACTORS

'Detractors' are the people who give a rating of six or below. They are not particularly delighted by the product or the service. They, without likelihood, won't purchase again from the company, could potentially harm the company's reputation through harmful word of mouth.

PASSIVES

'Passives' are the people who give the company a seven or eight got what they paid for, nothing more. They are fairly satisfied but could simply switch to a competitor's offering if given the opportunity. They probably wouldn't spread any negative word-of-mouth, but are not excited about company's products or services to actually promote them.

PROMOTERS

'Promoters' are the people who respond with a nine or ten are signaling that their lives have been enriched by their relationship with the company. They love the company's products and services. They are the replicate buyers, are the enthusiastic evangelist who recommends the company products and services to other potential buyers.

Net Promoter Score Brochure

Net Promoter Score (NPS) is a powerful tool in gauging customer loyalty and, by extension, company health.

Increase Revenue through Customer Experience Improvement

| 0 | 1 | 2 | 3 | 4 | 5 | 6 | 7 | 8 | 9 | 10 |

Not likely to Recommend   Extremely likely to Recommend

$$NPS = \% \, \smiley - \% \, \frownie$$

Table No. 4.2.1 showing NPS calculation.

	Amazon	Flipkart	Snapdeal	Homeshop18	Myntra	Jabong	e-Bay
Distractor	15.6%	15.3%	48.1%	81.0%	33.8%	67.3%	49.7%
Passive	29.9%	35.1%	30.5%	11.8%	28.6%	24.2%	26.1%
Promoter	54.5%	49.6%	21.4%	7.2%	37.7%	8.5%	24.2%
NPS %	39%	34.3%	-26.6%	-73.9%	3.9%	-58.8%	-25.5%

4.2.2 Graphical presentation of NPS

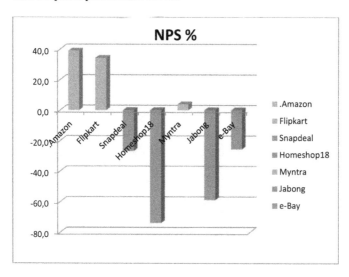

Interpretation

Amazon &Flipkart's net promoter score (NPS) is good, that means Amazon &flipkart's are customer centric, they believe in delivery superior value to their customer. Customer of this two E-retailer is behaving like loyal customers, typically making repeated purchases and giving the company a large share of their spending. NPS is a key metric of customer satisfaction. They talk up the company to their friends and colleagues, just as their answer to the question implies.

Fast delivery is one of the best service Amazon &Flipkart are providing. Different payment options available in Amazon &Flipkart which made customers more satisfied and comfort for paying while purchasing product. Customers feeling more secured when purchasing through these portal because of different policies and services they have.

Digital marketing techniques like search engine marketing, links providing other website and advertisement also functioned well for promotion of this website.The service provided by Amazon & Flipkart is good and more scope of development is there for increasing the customer strength.

CHAPTER-5

5.1 Conclusion

5.2 Findings

5.1 Conclusion

The purpose of this study is to examine the customers' perception towards Online Shopping. The survey was an attempt to understand the factors influencing customers' perception towards online shopping considering 30 variables. The survey revealed the most important factors that can be taken into account to understand the Internet shopping (include Customer Service, Convenience, Experience, Value added service and Product related information).Based on the study it can be concluded that the internet has given a great means to the customer to have in a convenient way but there is certain parameter likes security, trust, safety etc. which need to be focused upon. Customer perception is an essential term which needs to be considered seriously by the company to know the attitude and behaviour to formulate the strategy accordingly in order to satisfy the customer. Respondents have shown positive behaviour towards online shopping and they found it to be very good and useful to carry out shopping through online portals. But still, there are certain respondents who do not find such service as good which the company needs to tackle positively.

5.2Findings

The present study is analyzed using factor analysis, Net Promoter Score, and frequency analysis.

Factor analysis representing the loading of 30 variables into five factors that helps in understanding the customers' perception towards online shopping that is(Customer Service, Convenience, Experience, Value added service and Product related information), from this study it is evident that out of the total extraction value of 53.994, the significant variability is found in the "customer service &convenience". Theresults of Cronbach's alpha for this attributes, were obtained as 0.779, and 0.696 respectively, whichis well above the permissible value of 0.5.

From the calculation of Net Promoter Score,Amazon &flipkart'shaving higher score of NPS, Customer of these two E-retailers is behaving like loyal customers, typically making repeated purchases and giving the company a large share of their spending. The frequency analysis shows that the most of the respondents among the sample who use online shopping belongs to the age group of 21- 30 years old people more often chose online shops because of a greater range of products.

CHAPTER-6

6.1: Limitations

6.2: Future Directions

6.1: Limitations

Following are the few limitations to this study:

- The sample size of 154 is small so there may be difference in the reality and the finding.
- Findings of the survey are based on the assumption that the respondents have given correct information.
- Since the respondents had to fill the questionnaire while busy with their hectic schedule, many people were reluctant to answer.
- The respondents may be subjected to bias.
- The time limitation is one of the factors which influence the study.

6.2: Future Directions:

- Another study can be undertaken with larger sample to know customer perception towards online shopping in India.
- Online shopping pattern of males or females can be undertaken in the future.
- Another sincere study can be undertaken for various categories. Like fashion products, electronics, books, or home& kitchen.

BIBLIOGRAPH

1. Aghekyan-Simonian, M., Forsythe, S., Suk Kwon, W., &Chattaraman, V. (2012). The role of product brand image and online store image on perceived risks and online purchase intentions for apparel. *Journal Of Retailing And Consumer Services, 19*(3), 325-331.

2. Darley, W., Blankson, C., &Luethge, D. (2010). Toward an integrated framework for online consumer behavior and decision making process: A review. *Psychology And Marketing, 27*(2), 94-116.

3. Dash, S., &Saji, K. (2008). The Role of Consumer Self-Efficacy and Website Social-Presence in Customers' Adoption of B2C Online Shopping. *Journal Of International Consumer Marketing, 20*(2), 33-48.

4. Fiore, A., Kim, J., & Lee, H. (2005). Effect of image interactivity technology on consumer responses toward the online retailer. *Journal Of Interactive Marketing, 19*(3), 38-53.

5. Ganguly, B., Dash, S., Cyr, D., & Head, M. (2010). The effects of website design on purchase intention in online shopping: the mediating role of trust and the moderating role of culture. *International Journal Of Electronic Business, 8*(4/5), 302.

6. Goswami, S., & Khan, S. (2015). Impact of Consumer Decision-making Styles on Online Apparel Consumption in India. *Vision: The Journal Of Business Perspective, 19*(4), 303-311.

7. Guo, X., Ling, K., & Liu, M. (2012). Evaluating Factors Influencing Consumer Satisfaction towards Online Shopping in China. *Asian Social Science, 8*(13).

8. Ha, S., &Stoel, L. (2009). Consumer e-shopping acceptance: Antecedents in a technology acceptance model. *Journal Of Business Research, 62*(5), 565-571.

9. Hasan, A., & Mishra, S. (2014). Key Drivers Influencing Shopping Behavior in Retail Store. *LBS Journal Of Management & Research*, *12*(2), 30.

10. :Kim, J., Fiore, A., & Lee, H. (2007). Influences of online store perception, shopping enjoyment, and shopping involvement on consumer patronage behavior towards an online retailer. *Journal Of Retailing And Consumer Services*, *14*(2), 95-107.

11. Koufaris, M., & Hampton-Sosa, W. (2004). The development of initial trust in an online company by new customers. *Information & Management*, *41*(3), 377-397.

12. Kumar, V., Anand, P., &Mutha, D. A Study on Trust in Online Shopping in Pune: A Comparative Study between Male and Female Shoppers. *SSRN Electronic Journal*.

13. Ling, K., Chai, L., &Piew, T. (2010). The Effects of Shopping Orientations, Online Trust and Prior Online Purchase Experience toward Customers' Online Purchase Intention. *International Business Research*, *3*(3), 63.

14. Park, C., & Kim, Y. (2003). Identifying key factors affecting consumer purchase behavior in an online shopping context. *International Journal Of Retail & Distribution Management*, *31*(1), 16-29.

15. Punj, G. (2012). Consumer Decision Making on the Web: A Theoretical Analysis and Research Guidelines. *Psychology & Marketing*, *29*(10), 791-803.

16. Swarnakar, P., Kumar, A., & Kumar, S. (2016). Why generation Y prefers online shopping: a study of young customers of India. *International Journal Of Business Forecasting And Marketing Intelligence*, *2*(3), 215.

17. Won Jeong, S., Fiore, A., Niehm, L., & Lorenz, F. (2009). The role of experiential value in online shopping. *Internet Research*, *19*(1), 105-124.

18. Hasan, A. and Mishra, S. (2014). Key Drivers Influencing Shopping Behavior in Retail Store. LBS Journal of Management & Research, 12(2), p.30.

19. Zhou Lina, DaiLiwei and Zhang Dongsong (2007). ONLINE SHOPPING ACCEPTANCE MODEL — A CRITICAL SURVEY OF CONSUMER FACTORS IN ONLINE SHOPPING. Journal of Electronic Commerce Research, VOL 8, NO.1.

20. Nalchigar, S. & Weber, I. (2012). A Large-Scale Study of Online Shopping Behavior. CoRR,

21. StephenAbel,(2003). The Emergence of Interdependent E-Commerce Constructs", Journal of Internet Banking and Commerce, 8(2), p.67

22. Burke, R.R. (2002), "Technology and the Customer Interface: What Consumers want in the Physical and Virtual Store", Journal of the Academy of Marketing Science, Vol.30 No.4, pp 411-32.

23. . Balasubramanian, S., Konana, P. and Menon, N.M. (2003), "Customer satisfaction in virtual environments: a study of online investing", Management Science, Vol. 49, No. 7, pp. 871-89.

24. Aamir Hasan&Subash Mishra, (2015): Key Drivers Influencing Shopping BehaviourIn Retail Store, The IUP Journal OfMarketing Management, Vol. XIV, No. 3. pp. 54-60

25. Shrivastava,Archana,(2011). Behavioural Business Intelligence Framework Based on Online Buying Behaviour in Indian Context: A Knowledge Management Approach", International Journal of Computer Application, 02(6), pp,3066- 3078.

26. KamineniRajeev,(2004). Web based shopping: The evolution and the global implications – An exploratory analysis from a consumer behavioural viewpoint", Journal of Internet Banking and Commerce ,9(1)

27. . Dasgupta, L.E.M. and Melliar-Smith, P, (2005). Dynamic Pricing for Time-Limited Goods in a Supplier-Driven Electronic Marketplace, Electronic Commerce Research, (5) pp. 267 – 292.

28. Almousamoudi,(2011). Perceived risk in apparel online shopping, *Canadian social science*,7(2), pp.23-31.

29. Li Na And Zhang Ping (2002). Consumer Online Shopping Attitudes AndBehavior: An Assessment Of Research, *Eighth Americas Conference on Information Systems*.3(8) p.508-517

Appendix I - Questionnaire

"Factors Influencing Customers' Perception towards Online Shopping"

Dear All, Greetings! I am conducting an exploratory research regarding Factors Influencing Customers' Perception towards Online Shopping. Your response is vital for this study. Please be assured that your responses are completely confidential and will be used for academic purpose only. There is no right or wrong answers. Please select an option what you think is your answer....... Thanks!

1) Do you prefer online shopping?

   a) Yes b) No

2) For about how many years have you been using the online shopping?

   a) Less than 1 year.   b) 1-2 years
   c) 3-4 years.   d) More than 4 years.

3) How much time you engage on online shopping platform while shopping?

   a) Less than 1 hour.   b) 1-2 hours.
   c) 3-4 hours.   d) More than 4 hours.

4) What's your Age?

   a) Below 21 years   b) 21-30 years   c) 31-40 years   d) above 40 years

5) What's your gender?

   a) Male   b) Female

6) What's your education?

   a) Graduate- General (B. A, B. Cometc.)

   b) Graduate - Professional (BBA, B.E., MBBS, etc.)

   c) Postgraduate and above - General (M.A. etc.)

   d) Postgraduate and above - Professional (MBA, PGDM, M.E. etc.)

   e) Other.

7) What is your occupation?

   a) Government Employee.

   b) Private employee.

   c) Self-employed.

   d) A homemaker.

   e) A student.

   f) Retired.

8) What's your monthly household income?

   (The total income earned by all members of the household)

   a) Less than Rs. 25,000   b) Rs. 25,001-50,000

   c)Rs. 50,001-75000   d) More than 75000

9) Choose which category you mostly prefer to shop online?

   a) Electronics   ☐

   b) Appliances   ☐

   c) Fashion   ☐

   d) Books   ☐

   e) Home& kitchen   ☐

   f) Health& personal care. ☐

10) Given below is a list of some attributes that customers looking for while shopping in online. Please select your response for each attribute given below where 1 Means 'not at all important, 2 Means 'unimportant ', 3 Means 'neither important nor unimportant', 4 Means ' important', And 5 Means 'most important'.

1. Convenience of buying anytime anywhere	1	2	3	4	5
2. Range of products	1	2	3	4	5
3. Price dynamism	1	2	3	4	5
4. Ability to compare products	1	2	3	4	5
5. Availability of Value for money products	1	2	3	4	5
6. Products matching online description	1	2	3	4	5
7. On time delivery of the products	1	2	3	4	5
8. Availability of International brands	1	2	3	4	5
9. Detailed view or image zooming	1	2	3	4	5
10. Size guides(picture, table & test)	1	2	3	4	5
11. Filter according to your preference	1	2	3	4	5
12. Availability of trendy products	1	2	3	4	5
13. Guarantee & Warranty associated with the offerings	1	2	3	4	5
14. Information and review	1	2	3	4	5
15. The overall website experience	1	2	3	4	5
16. The attractiveness of the shopping portal	1	2	3	4	5
17. The website is easy to navigate	1	2	3	4	5

18. Discount & Coupon	1	2	3	4	5
19. Gift wrapping facility	1	2	3	4	5
20. Images / videos of the products give a good sense of the actual product	1	2	3	4	5
21. Cash on delivery	1	2	3	4	5
22. Easy to contact the customer service staff via email or chat	1	2	3	4	5
23. Free shipping	1	2	3	4	5
24. The online support staff is responsive to your needs	1	2	3	4	5
25. Easy to replacement & return	1	2	3	4	5
26. Product tracking facility	1	2	3	4	5
27. Security of payment credentials	1	2	3	4	5
28. EMI facility	1	2	3	4	5
29. In time refund	1	2	3	4	5
30. Standard delivery option	1	2	3	4	5

11) How likely you are to recommend this following online shopping platforms to your family & friends.

(On the scale from 0-10, where0 being "not at all likely" and 10 being "most likely".)

Amazon	1	2	3	4	5	6	7	8	9	10
Flipkart	1	2	3	4	5	6	7	8	9	10
Snapdeal	1	2	3	4	5	6	7	8	9	10
Homeshop18	1	2	3	4	5	6	7	8	9	10
Myntra	1	2	3	4	5	6	7	8	9	10
Jabong	1	2	3	4	5	6	7	8	9	10
e-Bay	1	2	3	4	5	6	7	8	9	10

12) When was the last time you made a purchase at online store?
   a) In the last week
   b) In the last month
   c) In the last 3 months
   d) In the last year
   e) Over a year ago
   f) Have never purchased online

13) The last time you visited online store, did you..
   a) Buy exactly what you were looking for
   b) Buy something in addition to what you were looking for
   c) Buy something other than what you were looking for
   d) Buy nothing
   e) Other

14) In the last 12 months, how many times did you visit any online store?

    a) None   b) 1 - 2 times   c) 3 - 5 times

    d) 6 - 10 times   e)11 - 20 times   f) More than 20 times

15) The last time that you visited, why did you visit online store?

a) Just browsing

b) To buy something for myself

c) To buy a gift

d) Re-directed by another website

e) Other

16) How likely are you to shop at online store again?

a) Very likely

b) Somewhat likely

c) Neutral

d) Somewhat unlikely

e) Very unlikely

17) Did you use any of website customer support features? Select all that apply.

    a) Toll-free number   b) Chat   c) Help

    d) Frequently Asked Questions (FAQs).   e) E-mail inquiry   f) other

General Information:

a) Name:

b) Place:

c) Phone no.

Appendix II - Sample profile

Q1. Do you prefer online shopping?	Frequency	Percent (%)
Yes	145	94.2
No	9	5.8
Total	154	100%
Q2.For about how many years have you been using the online shopping?		
less than 1 year	23	14.9
1-2 years	54	35.1
3-4 years	52	33.8
more than 4 years	25	16.2
Total	154	100%
Q3.How much time you engage on online shopping platform while shopping?		
less than 1 hour	63	40.9
1-2 hours	73	47.4
3-4 hours	13	8.4
more than 4 hours	5	3.2
Total	154	100%
Q4. What's your Age?		
below 21years	31	20.1
21-30years	102	66.2
31-40years	17	11.0
above40years	4	2.6
Total	154	100%
Q5.What's your gender?		
Male	86	55.8
Female	68	44.2

Total	154	100%
Q6.What's your education?		
graduate-general (B.A, B.COM etc)	45	29.2
Graduate - Professional (BBA, B.E., MBBS, etc)	40	26.0
Postgraduate and above - General (M.A. etc	9	5.8
Postgraduate and above - Professional (MBA, PGDM, M.E. etc.)	50	32.5
Total	154	100%
Q7.What is your occupation?		
government employee	5	3.2
private employee	42	27.3
self employed	6	3.9
a homemaker	4	2.6
a student	97	63.0
Total	154	100%
Q8.What's your monthly household income?		
less than Rs.25000	42	27.3
Rs.25000-50000	56	36.4
Rs.50001-75000	23	14.9
more than 75000	33	21.4
Total	154	100%
Q9.Choose which category you mostly prefer to shop online?		
Electronics	66	42.9
Appliances	4	2.6
Fashion	67	43.5
Books	8	5.2

Home & kitchen	5	3.2
health & personal care	4	2.6
Total	154	100%
Q10.When was the last time you made a purchase at online store?		
in the last week	50	32.5
in the last month	55	35.7
in the last 3 months	32	20.8
in the last year	11	7.1
over a year ago	6	3.9
Total	154	100%
Q11.The last time you visited online store, did you?		
buy exactly what you were looking for	66	42.9
buy something in addition to what you were looking for	43	27.9
buy something other than what you were looking for	17	11.0
buy nothing	15	9.7
Other	13	8.4
Total	154	100%
Q12.In the last 12 months, how many times did you visit any online store?		
None	9	5.8
1-2 times	14	9.1
3-5 times	22	14.3
6-10 times	39	25.3
11-20 times	21	13.6
more than 20 times	49	31.8

Total	154	100%
Q13. The last time that you visited, why did you visit online store?		
just browsing	36	23.4
to buy something for myself	91	59.1
to buy a gift	17	11.0
re-directed by another website	4	2.6
Other	6	3.9
Total	154	100%
Q14.How likely are you to shop at online store again?		
very likely	71	46.1
somewhat likely	39	25.3
Neutral	39	25.3
somewhat unlikely	3	1.9
very unlikely	2	1.3
Total	154	100%
Q15.Did you use any of website customer support features?		
toll-free number	68	44.2
Chat	29	18.8
Help	31	20.1
frequently asked questions(FAQs)	10	6.5
e-mail inquiry	10	6.5
Other	6	3.9
Total	154	100%

.